Rock St Robbery

by Gareth P. Jones
Illustrated by Emma Levey

OXFORD
UNIVERSITY PRESS

In this story ...

Pip Squeak

Kit Bags

Pip and Kit run *Finders Squeakers* – a lost and found agency. They help return lost things to their owners.

Stevie Riff

Chapter 1
The Sound Waves

Pip was in the workshop when Kit charged in, slipped on a battery and fell over.

"Are you OK?" asked Pip.

"I'm better than OK!" Kit replied, rubbing his head. "Haven't you heard? Stevie Riff is coming to Tailton Arena tonight."

"Is Stevie Riff someone I should be <u>aware</u> of?" asked Pip.

Pip wondered if she should be <u>aware</u> of Stevie Riff. Does that mean she had already heard of him or not?

"He's only the lead singer of The Sound Waves ... one of the best bands in the world!" exclaimed Kit. "Can we go to the concert? Can we? Please! Can we?"

"OK," said Pip. "We can take the aeroplane. I've been looking for a reason to take it out. I've <u>developed</u> a new steering lever, and I want to test it."

The Sound Waves
Tonight!

Support band:
Electric Blues

To <u>develop</u> something means to improve or create something gradually. Why might Pip have <u>developed</u> a new steering lever? What might she have wanted to change about the old one?

Later that day ...

The engine roared as Pip pushed the steering lever forward to <u>avoid</u> a thick, grey rain cloud. The aeroplane shot under the cloud. Then Pip pushed the lever hard to the left, and they headed down towards Tailton Arena.

"The steering lever seems pretty good to me," said Kit, gripping the side of his seat.

Pip wanted to <u>avoid</u> the rain cloud. Can you think of another word or words that you could use here instead of 'avoid'?

Pip landed behind a large coach.

"It's The Sound Waves tour bus!" said Kit. "Stevie wrote the hit song 'Breaking Glass' whilst on board."

"Was it a *smash* hit?" joked Pip.

"Actually, it was their first number one," replied Kit. He held up a notebook and pencil. "I really want to get Stevie's autograph."

"Then let's go and see if we can find him," suggested Pip.

It was <u>frantic</u> backstage, as people rushed around preparing for the concert.

Kit's ears pricked up when he heard a voice say, "Who would have taken my guitar? I left it in the dressing room."

"It's Stevie Riff!" said Kit, hopping up and down with excitement.

A man in a red t-shirt and black jeans walked past. He was talking to a woman wearing a headset.

If the people preparing for the concert were <u>frantic</u>, how might they have been feeling?

"I can't play without my guitar!" said Stevie, looking distressed. "The Sound Waves won't be able to go on stage. We might have to cancel the concert!"

Stevie and the woman disappeared down a corridor. Kit turned to Pip.

"Cancel the concert!" said Kit in alarm. "We have to help Stevie find his guitar! It's red with black stripes."

"Cheer up," said Pip. "How hard can it be to find a red-and-black stripy guitar?"

Chapter 2
Clues

Tailton Arena was filling up with excited people, eager to see the bands.

Backstage, Pip turned to Kit. "What time does the concert start?" she asked.

"Electric Blues are the first band on. They will play at half past seven," replied Kit. "Then The Sound Waves start at nine o'clock."

Pip checked the clock. It was quarter past seven. "We'd better get looking," she said.

They scurried down a corridor, stopping at a door with a sign that said: DRESSING ROOM.

"This must be where Stevie last saw his guitar," said Pip.

Just then, the door swung open. A woman wearing a blue top walked out, clutching a guitar case in her hand.

Pip and Kit pressed themselves against the wall to <u>avoid</u> being seen, but the woman was in too much of a hurry to notice them.

"Do you think Stevie's guitar could be in that case?" asked Kit.

"It's unlikely," replied Pip. "The other band are here to *support* The Sound Waves, not steal from them. Still, just to be on the safe side, why don't you follow her while I check the room for clues?"

What did Pip and Kit do to <u>avoid</u> being seen?

Kit disappeared down the corridor while Pip scurried into the dressing room. On one wall there was a large mirror surrounded by light bulbs. Opposite this was an empty guitar stand.

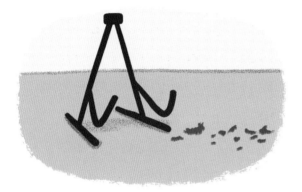

Pip noticed some flecks of blue paint on the carpet.

Next, she spotted a few clumps of dust.

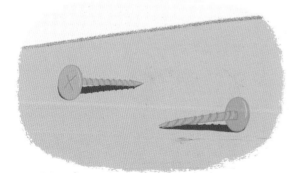

Then she saw a couple of screws.

Pip looked up and saw an open air vent directly above her. She opened her backpack and pulled out a small hook that was tied to a rope. She gave the rope a couple of swings, then threw it up into the air.

The hook caught on the vent. Pip pulled herself up. She slipped through the grate, gaining <u>access</u> to the dark, dusty air vent. Pip's footsteps echoed on the metallic floor as she hurried along the vent. Then she heard the sound of fluttering wings.

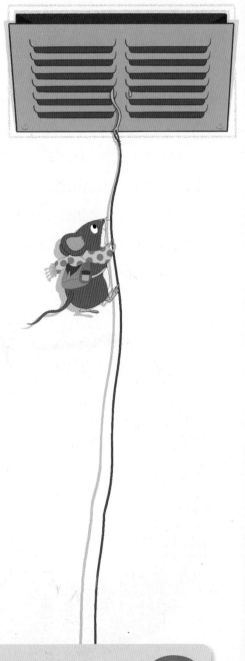

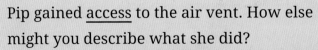
Pip gained <u>access</u> to the air vent. How else might you describe what she did?

Chapter 3
Electric Blues

Meanwhile, Kit had followed the woman to the stage. He held his breath as she opened the guitar case. He hoped to see Stevie's guitar, but to his disappointment the woman pulled out a blue guitar. She plugged it in and took her place on stage with her band.

"Ladies and gentlemen," said a voice through a loudspeaker, "it's time for Electric Blues!"

The crowd cheered as Electric Blues started playing music so loud that Kit had to put his paws over his ears. As he did so, he noticed something. High above the stage, a bird was perched on one of the lights. Kit's eyes widened as he realized it was a pigeon.

"Coo Lightfeathers," hissed Kit. "He must have something to do with the missing guitar."

Pip had also spotted the trouble-making pigeon. The air vent in the dressing room was <u>connected</u> to a vent above the stage.

"Don't move, Coo," ordered Pip.

"What?" said Coo, pretending not to be able to hear over the music.

"I said stop right there!" shouted Pip.

The air vent in the dressing room was <u>connected</u> to a vent above the stage. Does this mean that the vents joined up or not?

"I can't hear you!" squawked Coo.

Pip scurried along a thin metal beam towards Coo, but the pigeon hopped further away, on to another light. The light wobbled.

"Careful!" warned Pip.

Just then, the music stopped and the audience applauded wildly.

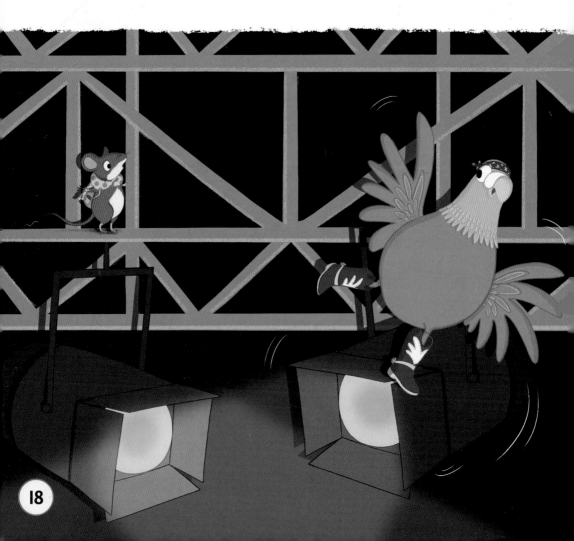

"Where's Stevie's guitar, Coo?" demanded Pip.

"Oh dear, is it missing?" Coo asked innocently. Then he gave a sly grin. "What a shame. That means he won't be able to go on stage. I will have to <u>trade</u> places with him!"

"You?" Pip said.

"Me." Coo puffed out his chest. "I will become the most famous rock star pigeon in the world!"

Coo wanted to <u>trade</u> places with Stevie. If you could <u>trade</u> places with someone famous for a day, who would it be?

"You'll never get away with this," said Pip.

"The only way to stop me is to find Stevie's guitar," replied Coo. "As you can see, I don't have it." Coo spread his wings and flew off. "Now I must go and get ready."

Chapter 4
Out of time

Electric Blues finished their final song and walked off to the sound of thunderous applause.

"We're out of time!" Pip thought.

The stage went black as the lights went out. While it was dark, Pip jumped from the high beam, then pulled a tag in her backpack that opened a parachute. She landed next to Kit.

"What's Coo up to?" asked Kit.

"Trying to steal the limelight as usual," replied Pip. She told Kit what Coo had said.

"He has no musical <u>ability</u>," said Kit crossly. "He just wants to be famous for the sake of it."

"Don't worry, we'll stop him!" said Pip. "What did you discover?"

"Nothing," admitted Kit miserably. "It was a blue guitar in that case."

An <u>ability</u> means you have a talent or skill.
Kit says that Coo has no musical <u>ability</u>. Which characters in the story do have musical <u>ability</u>?

Pip blinked. "Blue?"

"Yes," answered Kit. "Why?"

Pip's eyes gleamed. "I think I know what's happened," she said.

Chapter 5
Time to rock!

"Sound Waves ... Sound Waves ..." chanted the crowd in the arena.

Stevie Riff peered out at the crowd, looking worried. "Where *is* my guitar?" he said to himself.

Nearby, Pip and Kit had found the guitar case belonging to the Electric Blues' singer. Pip flicked the catch and opened the case. Inside, they found the blue guitar.

Suddenly, the stage lights came on and a voice boomed, "Ladies and gentlemen, prepare for the next big thing ..." It was Coo's voice. He was introducing himself.

Coo was standing on the other side of the stage. He was dressed in a sparkly red and gold suit, ready to make his big entrance.

Pip wasted no time. She gently scratched the guitar. A fleck of blue paint came off in her paw. She scratched some more, and red and black stripes started to appear under the blue paint.

"Stevie's guitar!" Kit gasped.

They quickly rubbed the rest of the blue paint off.

"We need to get Stevie's attention," Pip said. She jumped up on the guitar and strummed the strings with her paws. Then she and Kit ducked out of sight.

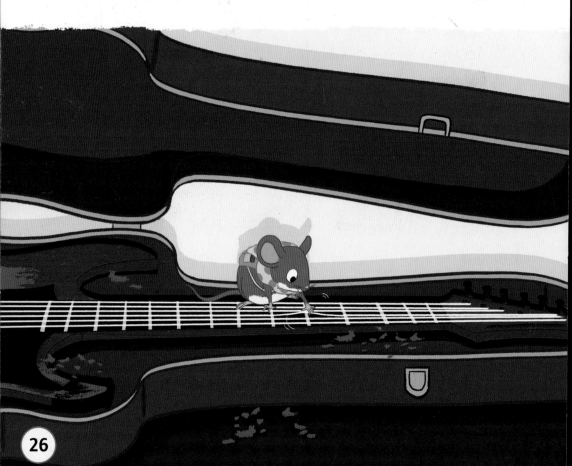

Stevie spun round. He hurried over to the guitar case. When he looked down, he saw his guitar and grinned. Then he picked it up, flung the guitar strap over his shoulder and strode out on to the stage with the rest of his band.

Chapter 6
Autograph

Everyone agreed that it was one of the best concerts
The Sound Waves had ever played.

Pip and Kit loved every minute.

After the show, they waited outside the stage door
for The Sound Waves to come out.

"How did you know it was the same guitar?" Kit
asked Pip.

"I saw blue paint in the dressing room," said Pip.
"Coo must have slipped through the vent and painted
the guitar so Stevie wouldn't recognize it. Coo painted
it blue because he knew the Electric Blues' singer
would mistake it for her guitar."

"All this so Coo could be famous?" said Kit.

"Yes," said Pip, "but luckily we were here to stop him."

Just then, the stage door opened and The Sound Waves came out. Kit waved his notebook in the air as Stevie began signing autographs.

"Happy?" asked Pip, as they headed back to their aeroplane.

"Yes!" Kit said, hugging his signed notebook. "There's no way I'm ever parting with this."

Pip smiled. She felt happy, too. Together they had solved the case of the rock star robbery.

Read and discuss

Read and talk about the following questions.

Page 3: Pip was not <u>aware</u> of Stevie Riff. How did Kit make her <u>aware</u> of him?

Page 4: If something <u>develops</u>, it changes or gets better. Have you ever <u>developed</u> something, for example a story or a picture?

Page 5: If you want to <u>avoid</u> something, do you go near it or keep away from it?

Page 7: What is the opposite of being <u>frantic</u>?

Page 14: How do you gain <u>access</u> to your home?

Page 17: Can you think of another way to say that something is <u>connected</u> to something else?

Page 19: Have you ever <u>traded</u> anything with a friend? What was it, and why did you <u>trade</u> it?

Page 22: Can you describe something you have the <u>ability</u> to do? What are you good at?